One-Minute Prayers™

To Start Your Day

Text by Hope Lyda

HARVEST HOUSE PUBLISHERS

EUGENE, OREGON

ONE-MINUTE PRAYERS™ TO START YOUR DAY
Copyright © 2005 by Harvest House Publishers
Eugene, Oregon 97402

ISBN-13: 978-0-7369-1615-8
ISBN-10: 0-7369-1615-6

Printed in the United States of America

06 07 08 09 10 11 12 / BP-CF / 12 11 10 9 8 7 6 5 4

Contents

Awake, My Soul

My heart is steadfast, O God,
my heart is steadfast;
I will sing and make music.
Awake, my soul!
Awake, harp and lyre!
I will awaken the dawn.

PSALM 57:7-8

Let the day dawn with music and celebration. I want to be a part of this rejoicing, Lord. You give my spirit cause for joy. Let my thoughts quickly turn to the blessings in my life so that my day begins with gratitude. Keep me from an attitude of defeat or mourning when I have been given this gift of another day.

Every minute is Yours. Please hear the music of my life. May it be pleasing to You and worthy of a new dance. Let my rejoicing bring the day from the night so that You will be praised and the world will see my light.

Beginnings

Facing the Day

At daybreak Jesus went out to a solitary place. The people were looking for him and when they came to where he was, they tried to keep him from leaving them. But he said, "I must preach the good news of the kingdom of God to the other towns also, because that is why I was sent."

LUKE 4:42-43

God, as I face a new day, help me be mindful of what You have planned. May my focus stay on Your desires so that I do not give my time, myself, and my day to other paths or work. Grant me discernment so I can recognize when a distraction is truly an indication of Your leading and not something to avoid.

It is not easy to turn my life over, even to You. But knowing that there is a purpose for me ahead, just minutes from now and as my day unfolds, I am excited to see what today might bring.

Inviting Wisdom In

The fear of the LORD is the beginning of wisdom, and knowledge of the Holy One is understanding.

PROVERBS 9:10

I like to act as if I know what I am doing most of the time—even when I am clueless. But Lord, this can get me into trouble. Help me seek Your wisdom and leading in more circumstances. May I begin with Your wisdom before stepping forth into this day and onto the path of my life.

My desire to know and understand my world and the people and situations in it will only be realized when I know You intimately.

A Day's Birth

I rise before dawn and cry for help; I have put my hope in your word. My eyes stay open through the watches of the night, that I may meditate on your promises.

PSALM 119:147-148

The hope I have in You is the beginning of my possibilities, my dreams, my future. Today is the beginning of the rest of my calendar of days. May I openly face all that You have for me. I wonder who You will place in my path. Will I find an open door where I least expect it? Will one step forward today be the start of something great and of Your hand?

I meditate on Your promises, Lord. They fill my heart and mind throughout the night. Now let me put my faith in those promises as a new day is born.

Giver of Life

*From birth I have relied on you; you brought me forth
from my mother's womb. I will ever praise you.*

PSALM 71:6

When I could not yet form words that made sense
to those around me…when I was unable to feed myself,
walk, or consider consequences of my actions, You
were my source of care and protection. You brought me
into this world, and now You bring me through this life.
I praise You for today. I even thank You for the trials I
face. When I am misunderstood at home or at work,
or I find I have made a faulty choice, I know You are
here for me.

You are the One who was with me at my beginning
and will be the One to embrace me at the end of my
days. Thank You for Your presence and comfort every
day in between.

Opportunity

Responding in Kind

Therefore, as we have opportunity, let us do good to all people, especially to those who belong to the family of believers.

GALATIANS 6:10

Soon after I called on You for grace, I turned around and was grumpy with someone who was trying to help me. I blamed this person for my day even though he was only trying to do his job. When will I learn to follow Your lead and honor all people? God, help me seek joy. Better yet, help me create joy in all circumstances.

I see today as a chance to serve others, to treat strangers and family with respect and kindness...and I see opportunities to put into practice the gift of grace in place of grumpiness, discomfort, or frustration.

Not of My Doing

The race is not to the swift or the battle to the strong, nor does food come to the wise or wealth to the brilliant or favor to the learned; but time and chance happen to them all.

ECCLESIASTES 9:11

Oh, how I would love to claim responsibility for the opportunities I have either made or taken advantage of. This would give me a sense of great accomplishment and power. But Lord, I know my good fortune is often the result of time and chance and Your goodness. I am the recipient of Your power—blessings shape my days.

When opportunity knocks, grant me the perspective and vision to see past my ego so that I understand my role was merely to turn the knob, open the door, and welcome it in. You made it, delivered it, and allowed me to recognize it.

With God

Jesus looked at them and said, "With man this is impossible, but with God all things are possible."

MATTHEW 19:26

I love to feel in control. Self-reliant. And exuding a sense of independence is a must. At least, this is what I project to the world. Truthfully—and You already know this—I depend on You for everything. Right before that meeting, I was praying for the right words and the courage to face the unknown. Before I made a decision that would impact my family, I was on my knees seeking Your will.

Lord, let me show others that You are my source of strength. Give me the confidence in You to stop keeping my weaknesses a secret. The more truth I reveal, the better I will reflect the One who makes the weak strong and the impossible possible.

Shape My Life

But the pot he was shaping from the clay was marred in his hands; so the potter formed it into another pot, shaping it as seemed best to him.

JEREMIAH 18:4

Yesterday was a bit of a bust, Lord. My big plans withered and my high hopes tumbled. My perfect, whole, flawless plan, once in the light of day, turned out to have cracks galore. So here I am, facing a new day and wanting it to be so much more. I have learned. This day I will give over to the Potter's hands so that You can best shape it.

I cannot wait to see what a day molded and prepared by You will look like. I believe it will be strong, beautiful, and whole.

Productivity

Seeing Your Purpose

*Blessed are all who fear the LORD, who walk in his
ways. You will eat the fruit of your labor; blessings
and prosperity will be yours.*

PSALM 128:1-2

I am in awe of You, Lord. And the more I understand Your greatness and the extent of Your power, the
better able I am to give my day over to You. Help me
see that to walk in Your way is the path to purpose and
meaning. I want each day to count. Let the next 24
hours serve You. Move me toward my personal best to
bear fruit that is pleasing to You.

Give me an understanding of productivity and purpose through Your eyes, Lord. Then when I face a
detour or a distraction, I will see it for what it is—a
chance to follow Your lead and be fruitful.

Giving Myself Over

Be diligent in these matters; give yourself wholly to them, so that everyone may see your progress.

1 TIMOTHY 4:15

Giver of life, grant to me passion and energy for all that I take on. Keep me bound to Your Word so that I am truthful and show integrity in all that I do. My schedule today includes difficult tasks. Help me to be diligent and mindful so others will see the work of Your hand. And when I face the projects that seem mundane, let me see their worth.

God, I want to be a contributor in all that I do. Give me strength to give every moment my very best. In my times of reflection, meditation, and prayer, may I give one hundred percent of my effort as these are offerings to You, Lord.

Legacy of Peace

LORD, *you establish peace for us; all that we have accomplished you have done for us.*

ISAIAH 26:12

Sometimes it takes chaos for me to better understand peace. When I am in the midst of circumstances that seem out of control or volatile, I can feel a stillness deep within that allows me to still seek You. I am sensing Your peace. When rough times are smoothed over and I am able to accomplish a goal, I know I have witnessed Your peaceful protection.

You do so much for me, Lord. Without You, I am without direction and purpose. Without You, I could not achieve anything of eternal value. Thank You, God, for caring for Your child.

Up to the Task

However, I consider my life worth nothing to me, if only I may finish the race and complete the task the Lord Jesus has given me—the task of testifying to the gospel of God's grace.

ACTS 20:24

Is today the day I will learn to be an example of Your grace, Lord? I hope so. I know that I have fallen short in the past. I start out with good intentions, but quickly drop them so I can reach for whatever suits me. Money. Success. Reputation. Status. These might reflect blessings from above, but they do little to share Your grace with those around me.

If I want to look back upon my days with pleasure, I need to be productive as a servant, a helper, a caregiver, a friend, and a sharer of the gospel of Your grace.

Others

Full of Grace

Be wise in the way you act toward outsiders; make the most of every opportunity. Let your conversation be always full of grace, seasoned with salt, so that you may know how to answer everyone.

COLOSSIANS 4:5-6

Open my ears to the needs of others, Lord. Let today be my chance to really hear what is being said by those around me. Often my personal agenda fills my mind as others express their hearts. Grant me patience, openness, and compassion so I will be eager to understand others needs. Perhaps they will just need to be listened to, maybe they will need comfort, or they might need to know of Your goodness.

After listening, may I speak words that are of You and intended for that particular person. Never let my own objectives override the conversation You intend.

Righteous Way

Do not repay anyone evil for evil. Be careful to do what is right in the eyes of everybody. If it is possible, as far as it depends on you, live at peace with everyone.

ROMANS 12:17-18

Cover me, Lord, as I go into my day. Protect me from my own desire to be right or to have my way. When I face someone who is not fair or just, give me the gift of silence or wise words to diffuse the situation. I'll admit, sometimes I would rather prove someone wrong than prove peace is righteous.

Lead my mind to peaceful solutions. Give my heart the tenderness it needs to see beyond evil to the needs of the oppressed. And bless me, Lord, with the presence of mind to act in a righteous way that gives others a glimpse of You, the Peacemaker of the soul.

Giving Out of Your Love

If someone forces you to go one mile, go with him two miles. Give to the one who asks you, and do not turn away from the one who wants to borrow from you.

MATTHEW 5:41-42

I cannot believe how much others expect of me. Today I will face the demands of family, coworkers, and others who need my time. When I answer my door, I know it will be someone who wants something from me. Save me from my first reaction, which is to shut down, or shut that door. Allow me to go above and beyond what people are asking of me. You will give me the strength and ability to do so. I need not worry about my own shortcomings.

Today, I will come to You and ask to borrow the patience, kindness, and love I need to go that extra mile.

Serving the Gifts

Each one should use whatever gift he has received to serve others, faithfully administering God's grace in its various forms.

1 PETER 4:10

I love gifts! I just am not sure which ones I have, Lord. Give me Your understanding of who I am in You. Allow me to see the gifts You have built into my heart and soul so that I can use this day for good. There are moments when I see my strengths in action, but I am not always consistent. Help me see the areas in my life that should be developed. Encourage me to let go of those activities or interests that are just taking time away from what You would have me do.

I want to get the most out of this life You have given to me, Lord.

Sacrifice

Leaving It All Behind

Peter answered him, "We have left everything to follow you! What then will there be for us?"

MATTHEW 19:27

I look around me and notice the absence of some things. While some luxuries or opportunities have been excluded from my world out of preference, some have been sacrificed so that I could live a life to better serve You and those I love. I am so thankful that I came to know You and the gift of Your grace. At that time, many unnecessary trappings and circumstances fell away from my life. Now I face each day hoping that I have pared my life down to the bare essentials.

God, You do not leave me wanting for anything. So please give me the courage and insight to leave behind all that I do not need in my life.

Take This Day

*I will sacrifice a freewill offering to you; I will praise
your name, O LORD, for it is good.*

PSALM 54:6

I pray to make this day a freewill offering to You.
As I rise and begin my morning, may I consider the
blessings around me so I will give You praise. May I
think about the people I will interact with so that my
heart will be prayerful. May I give decisions over to
You so I stay within Your will and move toward Your
purpose for me. May I observe the needs of others so
I can serve them as Your hands.

God, this day is Yours. I give it back freely so that
I might know You and Your ways better.

Acceptance Speech

When you sacrifice a thank offering to the LORD, sacrifice it in such a way that it will be accepted on your behalf.

LEVITICUS 22:29

I want to thank You, God, for providing me with a life of meaning and opportunity. When I forgot how to move through my days, You encouraged me through the kindness of others, Your Word, and glimpses of hope. Thank You for telling me the truth about Your love. You shared Your grace with my heart when I needed it most.

I wouldn't be where I am today if it weren't for You. There are many people to thank in my life, but I know the source of my understanding and my belief and inspiration is all You. Accept this heartfelt thanks—I offer You my thoughts, my work, and my praises all day long.

Change

Like a Child

And he said: "I tell you the truth, unless you change and become like little children, you will never enter the kingdom of heaven. Therefore, whoever humbles himself like this child is the greatest in the kingdom of heaven.

MATTHEW 18:3-4

How can I change my day today, Lord? In what ways do my grown-up thoughts keep me from embracing the pure, sincere faith of a child? Sometimes I think my goals hold me in a pattern of self-sufficiency, and I become unable to ask for help—even from You. My pride, my strong desire to find my own way as an adult keeps me from bowing down at Your feet and asking for Your guidance and mercy.

Show me today how to give up control and accept the changes—blessings and trials—that come with a humble, childlike faith.

Shape Me

*The Spirit of the Lord will come upon you in power,
and you will prophesy with them; and you will be
changed into a different person.*

1 SAMUEL 10:6

I give over my life to You this day. I submit my will
to Your will. By releasing my agenda into Your hands,
I will have the opportunity to see Your power at work
in my life. Where there is resistance, grant me peace so
that I can let go. Where there is doubt, grant me understanding so that I might become wise. Where there is
weakness, grant me wisdom so that I might defer to
Your strength.

God, every day I walk in faith should be a day to
allow You to change me, shape me, and create in me
the potential You planted in me.

Let Me Be Consistent

He who is the Glory of Israel does not lie or change his mind; for he is not a man, that he should change his mind.

1 SAMUEL 15:29

When I am not riding the fence with a decision, I am often wishing I had made another choice. My feet never seem to be on the firm ground of unwavering faith. I question everything and everyone because of my own faulty reasoning. God, help me focus on the path You have for me. Let my decisions be weighed against Your Word and will…and then let me have peace as I move forward.

You are consistent, honest, and true. May the first decision I make every day be to follow Your lead.

What Matters

Command those who are rich in this present world
not to be arrogant nor to put their hope in wealth,
which is so uncertain, but to put their hope in God,
who richly provides us with everything for our enjoy-
ment.

1 TIMOTHY 6:17-18

Direct me to invest my time and energy today into
matters of the heart. Steer me from tagging value to
temporal things of this world. You provide all that I
need. When will I learn that my job is not to build an
empire—my job is to serve the kingdom. It seems that
I have spent a lot of my daydreams envisioning a life
of status and carefree luxury when my time would be
better spent imagining how I might encourage others,
aid the poor, be sensitive to the wounded.

Remove my arrogance and replace it with a changed
heart of humility. I will be watching for ways to place
my hope in You.

Devotion

Hear My Wailing

Hezekiah turned his face to the wall and prayed to the LORD, "Remember, O LORD, how I have walked before you faithfully and with wholehearted devotion and have done what is good in your eyes." And Hezekiah wept bitterly. [And the LORD said,] "I have heard your prayer."

2 KINGS 20:2-3,5

I pray that my life is worthy of Your goodness. I value my relationship with my Creator and long to walk faithfully beside You. I have felt deep sorrow in my life, yet I have always known that You hear my cries. I pray my desire to do right and to live honorably will be pleasing to You. When my trials cause me to have doubts, may I also recall the times I cried out for help.

Remembering times of emotion inspires my devotion.

Focusing on Truth

The works of his hands are faithful and just; all his precepts are trustworthy. They are steadfast for ever and ever, done in faithfulness and uprightness.

PSALM 111:7-8

My thoughts pull me in many directions. When I turn to Your precepts, Your truths, I become focused and committed. I can pass through my days in a fog until I am confronted with a situation that needs attention and prayer. This is when I step out of my routine, my cruise-control mode, and step into my real life. I love this time. I feel Your love, I sense Your guidance, and I embrace Your faithfulness.

I am the work of Your hands. Forgive me when I forget this, Lord. Return me to situations that require the urgency of prayer and the desire to seek Your truth.

The Limitation of Need

*No servant can serve two masters. Either he will
hate the one and love the other, or he will be devoted
to the one and despise the other. You cannot serve
both God and Money.*

LUKE 16:13

As I rise and face my day, I notice that my thoughts
go to my financial needs. Not that I am planning major
corporate takeovers, but I am dwelling on the daily
ups and downs of my checking account. I feel the
worry start to consume me until I can wrap my mind
around a solution. I'm starting to realize how this focus
takes me away from serving the One I call my Master.

Clear away this clutter. I want my waking thoughts
to be devoted to You and Your priorities. I give You
complete control of my financial well-being. Let me
feel the freedom of this choice.

Heart and Soul

Now devote your heart and soul to seeking the LORD
your God.

1 CHRONICLES 22:19

From this moment on, I give my heart and soul
over to my Caretaker. You made me. You know me.
And You love me. I want to be a loyal follower who
always seeks Your face. When You shine Your grace
upon my day, it becomes a brilliant offering of
hope…not because of anything I have done, but
because You give my ordinary life eternal value.

I wonder where I will find You during my day. The
more I seek things of You, the more I will notice Your
hand on my life.

Commitment

The Arc of a Promise

*I establish my covenant with you: Never again will
all life be cut off by the waters of a flood; never again
will there be a flood to destroy the earth.*

GENESIS 9:11

Through the smear of water on my windshield
today, I could just make out the road ahead. The wipers
cut into my field of vision, and the rhythm of their
motion lulled me into deep thoughts. Funny how
moments like this bring me to questions about my life.
Either I have concern about my day ahead or I have
unfounded worries tied to my unknown future. But
just as I pulled into a parking lot, I saw a brilliant
rainbow framing the landscape beyond my reach. What
a glorious reminder that You are committed to my
today and to the days that are out of my reach.

As I thank You for the beauty of such colors against
a dark sky, may I remember all the times You carried
me from the floods of despair to the highlands of mercy.

Knowing Is Believing

Know therefore that the LORD your God is God; he is the faithful God, keeping his covenant of love to a thousand generations of those who love him and keep his commands.

DEUTERONOMY 7:9

You are God. You are the God of Adam and Eve. Your hands shaped the universe and every particle within its limitless mass. Every generation that has gone before has felt the presence of Your power. I am following in the footsteps of people who have witnessed Your love and care. Their stories remind me of Your commitment to all of Your creation.

When I feel lost in the swirl of the cosmos, I can grab onto the certainty of this commitment. In turn, my daily commitment to You—to keep Your commands—tethers me to the anchor of faith.

Words of Honor

Simply let your "Yes" be "Yes," and your "No," "No";
anything beyond this comes from the evil one.

MATTHEW 5:37

Recently I offered a halfhearted "yes" instead of sticking with my intended response of "no." Other times I will decline the very thing I should be agreeing to. Help me make wise decisions, Lord. If my unwillingness to do something can be traced to laziness or lack of compassion, then lead me into a solid "yes." When a decision could distract me from the priorities You have for me, give my voice strength as I say "no."

I long to clearly discern the Holy Spirit's leading. Make me sensitive to Your calling on my life so that my answers and path can be straight and true.

I Give You This Day

*Commit to the LORD whatever you do, and your
plans will succeed.*

PROVERBS 16:3

Every moment that unfolds today is Yours. I
commit my thoughts, my actions, my reactions, and my
plans to You. I pray for Your blessing upon my life, and
I seek Your strength when I face difficulties that might
tempt me to falter from Your way.

When I begin to think "this is just any ol' day," give
me a clearer sense of how great this day can be. My
offerings, small and large, can be used by You to turn
the next 24 hours into a great future.

Hope

Finding Purpose in Hope

May integrity and uprightness protect me, because my hope is in you.

PSALM 25:21

With hope in my heart, I am stronger and lighter. A soul affected by hope is no longer bound to the weight of everyday transgressions. Hope gives wings to my dreams and inspires me to goodness. With your help, I can step up to a task with integrity and honesty. When the daily grind feels redundant, my hope in You helps me clearly see the purpose that is before me.

So much will be born out of hope today. May I recognize the gifts of security and faith and use them to hold me up when nothing else will.

Hope Endures the Wait

We wait in hope for the LORD; he is our help and our shield.

PSALM 33:20

Today I will need help. No doubt about it. I seek You as my source of help and protection. Guide my steps, my words, my inclinations. I also have some burdens to give You. They are worries I have carried around for awhile. But rather than wait for something bad to materialize from these frets, I will wait for Your hope.

Knowing me, I will want to visit my worries from time to time. It is not easy to change my ways. Nevertheless, I trust in You. And I welcome hope into my life now that there is plenty of room.

Holding Fast

Let us hold unswervingly to the hope we profess, for he who promised is faithful.

HEBREWS 10:23

I can never make up my mind when ordering from a menu. A part of me wants everything listed. The other part of me is scared that as soon as I make my choice, I will realize it was the wrong one. God, don't let me be this way with my profession of hope. Let my belief in Your promises be strong, decisive, and complete.

Life offers many choices. And with each one, there is a risk. But my hope in You, Lord, is never a risk.

A Life of Hope

Be joyful in hope, patient in affliction, faithful in prayer. Share with God's people who are in need. Practice hospitality.

ROMANS 12:12-13

This week, I would love to be a spokesperson for hope. Not in billboard and commercial kinds of ways, but in gentle, subtle ways. Let me translate the hope I receive through faith so others can discern it. Grace me with kind speech and a willing spirit.

When I can step away from my selfish concerns and see the needs of others, I will fully embrace the intention of hope.

Provision

Turning First to You

*I sought the LORD, and he answered me; he delivered
me from all my fears.*

PSALM 34:4

When I seek You during my day, I will be reminded
that You are the source of all that I need. Instead of
looking to others to make my way easier, I will seek
Your wisdom and strength. Instead of relying on my job
to build me up, I will seek an identity grounded in
You. Each time a need surfaces, let my thoughts go to
You, my Creator.

Today I will encounter many opportunities to
receive from You. May I be mindful each time Your
provision protects me, covers me, and nurtures me.

What Comes from You

The LORD said to Moses, "I have heard the grumbling of the Israelites. Tell them, 'At twilight you will eat meat, and in the morning you will be filled with bread. Then you will know that I am the LORD your God.'"

EXODUS 16:11-12

How many times have You met my cries for help with perfect provision? And how many of those times have I not even noticed? Lord, give me eyes to see what comes from Your hand. My grumblings go on for so long that I have no voice left with which to praise You, and yet You still extend mercy.

Turn my whining into rejoicing. May every gift I receive from You be an opportunity to tell others of Your provision and forgiveness.

A Cause for Goodness

Our people must learn to devote themselves to doing what is good, in order that they may provide for daily necessities and not live unproductive lives.

TITUS 3:14

I know that before the day is over, I will have labeled numerous things "good." My morning latté, a conversation with a friend, a new recipe, a television show. But what will come from my lips, my hands that is truly good in Your eyes, Lord? I pray to have a day filled with goodness that affects people. I pray that my productivity moves me forward in Your will.

Devotion is not a word used too much these days. But I hope I can take on a spirit of devotion as I discover ways to bring goodness to light and to honor goodness when it crosses my path.

May I Have a Miracle?

*God gave Solomon wisdom and very great insight,
and a breadth of understanding as measureless as
the sand on the seashore.*

1 KINGS 4:29

I don't feel very wise today. Just the act of getting dressed and heading out the door was draining, and now I am supposed to head into my day with purpose. God, expand my spirit, my heart, and my soul so that I can take in every bit of wisdom and understanding You give me. Stretch my sense of knowledge so I will have a heavenly perspective about what truly matters.

On days like this, when it seems a miracle for me to function, I pray for the provision of godly perspective. When I quit trying to be wise and learn to rest in Your ways, I do believe life will open up in extraordinary ways. May this be the day I make that so.

Perseverance

Making It Through

So do not throw away your confidence; it will be richly rewarded. You need to persevere so that when you have done the will of God, you will receive what he has promised.

HEBREWS 10:35-36

"If I can just get through this...."

I find myself repeating this statement often. I look for the silver lining that will make a current task tolerable. My eyes scan the horizon for the crossroads that will offer me an alternative to the burden of today. Perseverance is a requirement of faith. I thank You for this part of the journey because I believe perseverance is also a gift.

When I do get through whatever is on my plate for today, I know I will receive the promises You have for me. If I do not know the sweat of the work, I will never know the sweetness of the victory.

Love One Another

Keep on loving each other as brothers.

HEBREWS 13:1

Lord, help me. Today I will encounter a person who usually causes me to stumble. I get defensive in his presence. I'm not even myself when he enters the room. Why do I allow my emotions to get the best of me and turn a situation from good to bad? I am giving this situation over to You. And I am asking to see this person through Your eyes rather than through my tainted lens of past experiences.

I feel good about this. I have never turned my interactions with this person over to the power of prayer. Now I will persevere in Your strength and not my own…and that will change everything.

Gift of Compassion

As you know, we consider blessed those who have persevered. You have heard of Job's perseverance and have seen what the Lord finally brought about. The Lord is full of compassion and mercy.

JAMES 5:11

My mind goes to several friends today, Lord. They all are in need of Your healing touch. Their journeys are filled with great difficulties. The darkness of fear covers their thoughts even as they pray for hope. I pray that their perseverance leads them to blessings You will bring about. In their pain, You offer compassion and comfort. In their worry and uncertainty, You offer mercy.

I want to be a friend who encourages. Give me Your words as I speak to my friends and lift them up in prayer.

Contentment

Open for Joy

Create in me a pure heart, O God, and renew a steadfast spirit within me....Restore to me the joy of your salvation and grant me a willing spirit, to sustain me.

PSALM 51:10,12

Let today be a clean slate that welcomes the hope and joy ahead, Lord. I no longer want to wake up to thoughts of many losses, mistakes, or "should've" scenarios. As soon as I begin that tally, the day's potential joy is already lost.

Restore to me the joy of my salvation when I felt the impact of a clean spirit. I was buoyed by the release of my burdens to Your care. I not only accepted joy but watched for it to be a part of my experience. Time and circumstances have jaded that view. Remind me of the contentment of faith.

Two Steps Forward...

But godliness with contentment is great gain. For we brought nothing into the world, and we can take nothing out of it. But if we have food and clothing, we will be content with that.

1 TIMOTHY 6:6-8

Why am I so quick to grab things? Stuff consumes me. It fills my home. My thoughts. My space. I don't even want most of these things. Even with a discerning mind in this head of mine, I have given myself over to the marketing monster. I consider this foolish behavior and, beyond that, I consider the acquisition of things as irrelevant to a worthy life. God, remove this lust from my heart so that godly contentment will again be a part of my journey.

Pare away the trivial so that I might truly see what is of Your hands. May I learn to recognize what resources You give me to use in this journey so that I might discover the life You intended for me.

What a Friend

You have made known to me the path of life; you will fill me with joy in your presence, with eternal plea-sures at your right hand.

PSALM 16:11

I am excited to think of spending time with a good friend today. We are able to talk about the real stuff of life and also give ourselves over to laughter that is true and deep. We're never self-conscious together. Lord, I know that in Your presence, You offer a friendship as vulnerable and joyful as this earthly one. I'm ashamed to say that I have forgotten this at times and have entered into Your presence like a scolded child rather than a person intending to experience the pleasures of being known and loved and cherished.

You carve out the path of my days through the history of time and experience. Help me step into the joy as well. And may I learn to rush into Your presence with great expectations for contentment and lasting relationship.

Giving It Over

Submit to God and be at peace with him; in this way
prosperity will come to you.

JOB 22:21

My restless spirit will not find peace until I come
to You and ask You to take all of my life and shape it
into being. You formed me in my mother's womb, yet
I still hold tightly to what I claim to be "mine,"
including victories and worries. This does not allow
me peace. Give me a glimpse today of what it means
to give myself over to You fully. Walk me through this
important lesson so I will release my grip.

Prosperity, trials, and the storms of life will be man-
ageable and even welcomed when I know they, too, are
under Your submission in my life. No longer will such
changes and circumstances cause my spirit to be anx-
ious and uncertain.

Now

The Covering of a Life

If that is how God clothes the grass of the field, which is here today and tomorrow is thrown into the fire, will he not much more clothe you, O you of little faith?

MATTHEW 6:30

As I get dressed for the day, I know that I am really facing the day naked and dependant upon You to clothe me. Your grace clothes me with forgiveness. Your mercy clothes me with compassion. Your love covers me with value. I do not make a decision during my day that does not rely on Your hand.

My faith has been small in many ways, but that was in the past. I want to outgrow that old faith so that I can be dressed in the faith You have for me now.

One Thing at a Time

Therefore do not worry about tomorrow, for tomorrow will worry about itself. Each day has enough trouble of its own.

MATTHEW 6:34

Slow me down, God. I use my energy each morning troubleshooting for the days ahead. I completely bypass the gift of today, the gift of now. Calm my spirit, expand my breaths, fill me with Your peace so that my spinning thoughts settle. I serve no greater good by thinking ahead, wringing my hands, and wondering what might happen.

Save me from my need to control every situation or possible situation. Lead me back to trusting You with all that will happen. I know that You do not ask me to handle everything on my own. You will be there with me, for me. So today, this moment is only about this moment. May I rest in it and experience it as You intended.

Seeking the Words

Whenever you are arrested and brought to trial, do not worry beforehand about what to say. Just say whatever is given you at the time, for it is not you speaking, but the Holy Spirit.

MARK 13:11

Give me the words I need. I have fretted over today's situation for some time now, and I realize how useless that worrying was. Just as You provide my daily bread, You will provide the words and thoughts I need when pressures exist. Remove the spirit of fear that sweeps over me. Allow me to listen to the Holy Spirit for my leading.

I can rework phrases in my head now and hope everything turns out later. Or I can keep my thoughts on You and know You will take care of me when the time comes.

Following Your Lead

*Love the LORD your God with all your heart and
with all your soul and with all your strength. These
commandments that I give you today are to be upon
your hearts.*

DEUTERONOMY 6:5-6

God, I want to use my many moments today to
love You completely. When I catch myself wandering
in thought, I will begin to praise You. When my day
lacks energy, I will pray for Your love to act through me.
Fill my soul with understandings of You and Your ways
so that my "now" is infused with Your presence.

Carve on my heart all that You hope for my life,
Lord. I will follow this map each step of the way.

Renewal

Finding You

If a man dies, will he live again? All the days of my hard service I will wait for my renewal to come. You will call and I will answer you; you will long for the creature your hands have made.

JOB 14:14-15

Whatever trouble today brings, I know the situation will be restored in Your time. I have great relief knowing that my hard times will be shaped into good things. All I need to do is remember my life before I met You and I understand what a new life is all about. Grace. Second chances. Renewal.

I long for You. The pace of my day might cause me to forget this, but in the quiet moments between sleep and wakefulness I feel the pull toward Your presence. And my joy deepens when I realize You long for me as well.

Shine

*Restore us, O L*ORD *God Almighty; make your face
shine upon us, that we may be saved.*

PSALM 80:19

Some days are just colder than others. I need to feel
the warmth of Your face shining upon me, Lord. I want
to be covered by Your radiance. Resting in the palm of
Your hand, I feel secure and saved. Lead me back to this
place.

Your promises will unfold as the day progresses.
And I will gather these even as I am uncertain about
how the day will play out because through Your promises come renewal and wholeness.

Resurrection's Power

We were therefore buried with him through baptism into death in order that, just as Christ was raised from the dead through the glory of the Father, we too may live a new life.

ROMANS 6:4

My personal resurrection seems to be taking place slowly. I know that You gave me a new life when I gave my heart to You, but Lord, sometimes I fall back into the ways of old. I want the renewal given to me by grace through Your resurrection. I want to see, taste, and feel what it means to live as a freshly conceived creation.

You carry me through the pain of death to the glories of life. Yet some days, like today, I do very little to follow You wholeheartedly. Your love—it surprises me. And just when I feel hopeless, You give me a sign of renewal. An idea. A song. A prayer. A friend. A hope. This is resurrection in motion in my life.

The Next New Thing

You were taught, with regard to your former way of life, to put off your old self, which is being corrupted by its deceitful desires; to be made new in the attitude of your minds; and to put on the new self, created to be like God in true righteousness and holiness.

EPHESIANS 4:22-24

People talk about new attitudes, new ways of thinking, new ways of being. I tried that in the past, and it was very difficult to maintain whatever new thing I was trying to incorporate into my life. I wanted others to identify me with this new choice, yet I wouldn't try it on long enough for this to happen.

It is only when renewal of the mind and spirit occurs that transformation takes place. My earlier changes were surface level, never intended to be life-changing. Only this choice I make to be Yours will result in a new self worth noticing.

Trials

When Trouble Comes

If any of you lacks wisdom, he should ask God, who gives generously to all without finding fault, and it will be given to him. But when he asks, he must believe and not doubt, because he who doubts is like a wave of the sea, blown and tossed by the wind.

JAMES 1:5-6

I find myself in a bit of a predicament, as You already know, I'm sure. This morning finds me facing some drama in my life. I have nobody to blame except myself. I denied Your wisdom even though You offered it to me. I turned my back on the leading of the Holy Spirit. This sounds all negative, but in truth, this situation has led me back to You. Every time I forget who really is in control, I end up playing a role in some silly dilemma that could have been avoided.

I would say "never again," but I have said that before. I will just say thank You for giving me the resources to work my way through this trial. And may I turn to You sooner than later next time.

Tuning In to You

I urge you, brothers, by our Lord Jesus Christ and by the love of the Spirit, to join me in my struggle by praying to God for me.

ROMANS 15:30

A tug on my heart this morning leads me to pray for my friends who are going through difficulties. I tuck them in my mind for thought throughout the day, but You know how busy the day becomes. Starting off my day by lifting up others in prayer tunes my heart to be prayerful and mindful of these people all day—even when busy.

Grant me a prayerful nature. It takes work for me to practice this discipline, Lord, yet it also offers me a closeness with You that I long for. I draw near to You right now and pray for myself and others that our trials will lead us back to You always.

Life Work Ahead

No discipline seems pleasant at the time, but painful. Later on, however, it produces a harvest of righteousness and peace for those who have been trained by it.

HEBREWS 12:11

How much work is required of me? Some days I think I am stuck on a treadmill rather than on a road that leads somewhere. What do You ask of me, God? I know that most often I am running to follow the commands that come from others, myself, and the world around me—and not from You.

Help me see that the good work I do will have a harvest of righteousness. And let me identify the work I am racing to complete that serves no purpose other than feeding my ego. Give me the strength to choose that which serves You.

Spiritual Student

*Come to me, all you who are weary and burdened,
and I will give you rest. Take my yoke upon you and
learn from me, for I am gentle and humble in heart,
and you will find rest for your souls. For my yoke is
easy and my burden is light.*

MATTHEW 11:28-30

If I can look at my current trial as a form of education, I can almost deal with all that it is costing me—time, energy, heartache, headaches. But this also means that I need to follow the way of my teacher. And You are my teacher for life. All that I need to know and learn comes from my source of life and grace.

Bring me into Your classroom every morning. When I sit at the back of the class, awaken my spirit and call on me, Lord. I am a pupil who needs to see what the Master has for me. You do not give me problems just for the sake of entertainment. You allow these problems so that I will come to You and ask for rest, guidance, and a lesson in faith.

Promise

Trust Takes Trial

*You know with all your heart and soul that not one
of all the good promises the LORD your God gave you
has failed. Every promise has been fulfilled; not one
has failed.*

JOSHUA 23:14

It is easy to forget all that You have brought me
through. Not because I am not grateful but because
after a fall, I am always quick to embrace life and goodness. I don't want to look back or dwell on the troubles
I have experienced. But I am realizing how important
it is to look at these times. They strengthen my journey.

Today, I begin a new kind of trial. I have never been
here before…not exactly. But all I need to do is recall
the promises You have planted in my spirit, and I trust
You once again. The good news—even if the trials are
not getting easier, the trusting is.

Resting in the Unknowing

As you do not know the path of the wind, or how the body is formed in a mother's womb, so you cannot understand the work of God, the Maker of all things.

ECCLESIASTES 11:5

I am clueless how today will turn out. Why do I even bother to guess, assume, or presume anything? I'm so ridiculous that way. Wanting to feign I am in control because times are hard. I cannot know the big picture. I do know You are the one for me to trust. I have examples of Your goodness and faithfulness in my life. I cling to these.

When people ask me what I am going to do or even why something is happening, I no longer want to fabricate my actions or make up reasons. I want to rest in the unknowing. I want to rest in the security of my Maker's plan, come what may.

The Power of a Plan

"For I know the plans I have for you," declares the LORD, "plans to prosper you and not to harm you, plans to give you hope and a future."

JEREMIAH 29:11

Is this really the way to go? Personally, I wouldn't have done things this way, but You are God and I am so very human. My vision is limited and failing. I tend to hold on to people or things that really are meant to be released. And I second guess everything. I'm not telling You anything You don't already know.

But do You know that today I woke up and felt excited about the plan You have for me? I have finally given myself over to the idea of the future being about hope and not fear. It's a new thing for me, but I think I could get used to it.

Awareness

Learning to Be Aware

Know also that wisdom is sweet to your soul; if you find it, there is a future hope for you, and your hope will not be cut off.

PROVERBS 24:14

Recently I have moved through my days in a bit of a fog. I look back on the past week, month even, and sense that I have not been aware of You and the lessons You would have me learn. I don't want to be someone who mentally checks out of life. Even when I face difficulties, I will glean wisdom that feeds my soul.

Make me aware of what You would have me learn today, Lord.

In the Wake of a Day

Hear, O Israel, and be careful to obey so that it may go well with you and that you may increase greatly in a land flowing with milk and honey, just as the LORD, the God of your fathers, promised you.

DEUTERONOMY 6:3

This morning I turned off my alarm, sat on the edge of the bed, and just listened to You. Before the flood of plans, thoughts, regrets, or schedule changes filled the space between my ears, I used my ears to take in Your directions.

I pray to be aware of what You ask of me so that I can obey faithfully. I want to walk in Your ways so that I can step into Your promises.

Me Me Me

*Hear and pay attention, do not be arrogant, for the
LORD has spoken.*

JEREMIAH 13:15

I never thought my pride could actually block me
from understanding You. But these days, I am stub-
born—always trying to figure out the way on my own.
I speak up on behalf of myself, my opinions, and my
ego more often than I speak up for my faith. I let my
concerns consume me before I turn to You in prayer.

So much me and so little You makes for a difficult
life. I miss Your gentle leading. My mind and heart are
too scattered to take in Your truths. I don't even taste
the simple joys because I deem them insignificant. Help
me strip away my own agenda and prideful ways so
that I have nothing blocking my view of You.

Taking Notice

Then he returned to his disciples and found them sleeping. "Could you men not keep watch with me for one hour?" he asked Peter. "Watch and pray so that you will not fall into temptation. The spirit is willing, but the body is weak."

MATTHEW 26:40-41

Will You catch me sleeping today instead of being alert? How many chances do I miss to do right, to do good, or to serve another? Please open my eyes to those I meet who need help that I can offer. Sharpen my mind so I can be discerning.

When I am tired, it is easy for me to fall back into old, bad habits. Grant me the energy to be careful and wise. When the wisdom I need is beyond my capacity, give me Your wisdom to see the way through a situation.

Courage

Carry Me

Let the morning bring me word of your unfailing love, for I have put my trust in you. Show me the way I should go, for to you I lift up my soul.

PSALM 143:8

I feel like such a child. Today gives me too much worry and grief and stress. I thought I could do it—carry out the day—but I cannot. I need You, God. I not only need You to be with me, but I need You to carry me through this day of mine. I started out so strong, but now that I face the reality of moving forward, I cannot go it alone.

Show me the way. I lift up my day to You and pray for courage to keep going. I trust You. And where there is still resistance to rely on You instead of myself, please remind me of this feeling in the pit of my stomach. You are my only source of strength.

Needing a Savior

Those who know your name will trust in you, for you, LORD, have never forsaken those who seek you.

PSALM 9:10

I come to Your presence today with a bit of a sheepish look and a heavy heart. I have been here before—countless times—and You have not forsaken me. But I feel so needy that sometimes I second-guess returning to You. But I know Your name, and You are my Holy Redeemer. You are my Savior and Messiah. It is grace that falls from Your lips, not a gavel of conviction when I am humble and in need.

God, grant me the peace that comes with Your strength and courage. Do not let me turn my back on You when I so desperately require Your guidance.

Returning to the Boat

Immediately he spoke to them and said, "Take courage! It is I. Don't be afraid." Then he climbed into the boat with them, and the wind died down. They were completely amazed.

MARK 6:50-51

Do I even recognize You when You enter my boat to calm the storms and save my soul? Have I ever looked past You as I watch for a Savior who seems bigger, stronger, and more able to pull me from the clutches of the waves? I know I have because my self-doubt can make my faith weak. Yet You are faithful each time, and my worries fade.

I do take courage in You. I will not look beyond Your shoulders to the night sky in search of more. I will trust You. You are the One who returns to the boat of my life and tells me not to be afraid.

Thirst

The Hunger of the Void

Blessed are those who hunger and thirst for righteousness, for they will be filled.

MATTHEW 5:6

Sometimes I skate over the voids in my life. I don't even look down to see if the chasm still exists because I don't want to know. But days like today I cannot get up without asking for You to fill that void. I know it is there, and I know I cannot skate, skip, or jump over it—even in a state of denial. The hunger comes from deep within and it does not fade when I puff up my own ego or worth.

My hunger and thirst leads me back to Your righteousness, Lord. Only You can fill this place that questions, that missteps, that becomes empty when ignored. Fill this place in me and let it overflow to all that I do and am.

Seeing the Answer

He humbled you, causing you to hunger and then feeding you with manna, which neither you nor your fathers had known, to teach you that man does not live on bread alone but on every word that comes from the mouth of the LORD.

DEUTERONOMY 8:3

When I ask You for wealth, what do You send instead? When I ask for bread, what nourishment do You bestow upon me and my family? When I lack, what do You give to me to make up for my weakness? All that carries me into my life and through it comes from Your hand and Your way of sustenance.

When my stomach growls, I may question what I see fall from heaven to fill my plate. But, Lord, I receive these gifts with faith and with the belief that You are guiding my journey—and You do not leave Your children to starve.

Beyond Reasons

For I was hungry and you gave me something to eat, I was thirsty and you gave me something to drink, I was a stranger and you invited me in, I needed clothes and you clothed me, I was sick and you looked after me, I was in prison and you came to visit me.

MATTHEW 25:35-36

The needs of my brothers and sisters around me are so great, I do not know where to start. There is a strong desire, a thirst to quench, to reach out and help others. But then I sit back and list the stipulations or the reasons this could go very wrong. This is when I think of You asking us to feed, clothe, and aid the sick, and visit the imprisoned, and it is clear You do not ask me to ask, You ask me to serve.

May I truly see You in those I will help today. And when I cannot, give me the strength to continue giving. Because even when I am blind to You, You are the one who stands before me asking for more.

Learning to Knock

*Ask and it will be given to you; seek and you will
find; knock and the door will be opened to you. For
everyone who asks receives; he who seeks finds; and
to him who knocks, the door will be opened.*

MATTHEW 7:7-8

Maybe I have lived through too many fund-raisers
as a kid to feel comfortable enough to stand in front of
a door and knock. I think about the possible rejection
and ignore the desire in me to know the One on the
other side. I consider other ways I could go about
asking for assistance—the phone, a letter, an e-mail…a
prayer—and they seem so much better suited to my
personality.

Lord, get my clenched fingers to start knocking.
The excuses rush over my good intentions like a tidal
wave. Yet I understand that first You require us to come
to You…humbled, seeking, and thirsty. This is when
You answer the door. But first, I must knock.

Responsibility

Living the Work

All hard work brings a profit, but mere talk leads only to poverty.

PROVERBS 14:23

I hit the snooze button on the alarm several times this morning. I started to pray and then ended up venting about the work I have to get done today. Now I'm back and thanking You for the work I have to do because I know it is a gift from You. My venting leads to nothing productive or fruitful. It only builds the toxic thoughts in my mind and heart.

But hard work has its own reward of faithfulness, results, labor, and sacrifice. It is also a chance for me to sense the thrill of creation—even if in a very minor way. Lord, take the work that is before me and shape it into a worthwhile effort. I have rolled up my sleeves, and I am now ready to receive this beneficial part of life.

Stay

Brothers, each man, as responsible to God, should remain in the situation God called him to.

1 CORINTHIANS 7:24

Surely You jest. This is what I am thinking sometimes as I head into the situation You have placed me in lately. This couldn't possibly be of God...of Your hand. Could it? Lord, give me perspective on this. Maybe I just want to avoid this kind of responsibility. It seems there is rarely a break from it. Maybe there are other lessons You want me to learn right now.

I will remain here because You remain beside me. I cannot do this alone. Please help me see inklings of the purpose of this time and place in my life. If not now, sometime soon. When I do not see the reason, please give me the inspiration.

Knowing Whom to Follow

Do not follow other gods, the gods of the peoples around you; for the LORD your God, who is among you, is a jealous God and his anger will burn against you, and he will destroy you from the face of the land.

DEUTERONOMY 6:14-16

In my covenant with You, I understand that I am responsible to You. My job is not to serve other gods of money, fame, or whatever else society dangles in front of me. My sole, or soul, responsibility is to honor and serve You. This accountability used to give me cause for worry. What if I cannot hold up my end of things? But now I see it as a wonderful tie to You, my Creator. I want to know that what I do has a purpose in Your eyes.

Grant me a strong sense of connection with You as I walk through my days and stay true to You. When my eyes fall to other gods, return me to Your presence so that I uphold Your name. It gives me joy that I am responsible to You because it means I am Yours.

Courage in Faith

Do your best to present yourself to God as one approved, a workman who does not need to be ashamed and who correctly handles the word of truth.

2 TIMOTHY 2:15

There is someone in my life who needs to hear about You. I need to see myself as worthy, as a child approved by You to share Your message of hope. My shyness overtakes my sense of responsibility to pass along what I know about my Maker. I'm not ashamed of You, but I am embarrassed about my lack of full knowledge about the things of faith.

Give me a spirit of strength and purpose so that I might find the words to start the conversation. May I offer what needs to be heard, and may I be a listener who reflects Your nature.

Direction

Show Me Your Will

Be very careful, then, how you live—not as unwise but as wise, making the most of every opportunity, because the days are evil. Therefore do not be foolish, but understand what the Lord's will is.

EPHESIANS 5:15-17

Discerning Your will is hard. I start my day asking for Your guidance so that I will make good decisions and follow the path You want for me. But by lunchtime I sense I have lost any sense of an inner tug. I rely on my knowledge of Your Word—and that carries me through situations, conversations, and many choices. But today I just want to know if I am close to being right in Your will.

Please direct me and my thoughts so I can look at my life through Your eyes and through Your heart. I long to walk with You all of my days.

Shape My Steps

In his heart a man plans his course, but the LORD determines his steps.

PROVERBS 16:9

I have big plans for my day. I will be productive, creative, efficient, and graceful as I accomplish so much. Okay, maybe my real plan is just to survive. But faith stretches my motives toward bigger purposes. I see how even the smallest acts can be turned into blessings. I realize my accidental moments might be part of Your intentional plans.

I just need to be facing the right direction—toward You.

The Release of Compassion

*Consider the blameless, observe the upright; there is
a future for the man of peace.*

PSALM 37:37

Sometimes my direction comes from within. Not only from Your guiding presence but from a driving force. I'm still looking for my personal passion, but lately I have felt led by the power of peace. My heart is more tender. Compassion comes more easily.

Where will this newfound sensitivity take me? How do You want it to impact my life? Show me how to allow more peace into my days, and I will take it with me into my future.

Purify My Heart

There is surely a future hope for you, and your hope will not be cut off. Listen, my son, and be wise, and keep your heart on the right path.

PROVERBS 23:18-19

Keep my path straight. I become easily distracted, but I want to stay on track. I pray that You will bring people into my life who will guide me when I do step off the intended route or become fascinated by the wrong map. Nudge me with ideas and things I read. Fill my mind with whatever it takes to steer me toward wisdom.

My prayer today is for purity. Save me from the clutter and mess that taints my viewpoint. I want to be free and willing to embrace the hope of my future.

Authenticity

Sharing the Real Me

The LORD detests lying lips, but he delights in men who are truthful. A prudent man keeps his knowledge to himself, but the heart of fools blurts out folly.

PROVERBS 12:22-23

Oh, Lord, help me be truthful today. No more gossip or little white lies. No more hedging my answers to pacify people or to sway arguments. I want to be authentic in my speech, thoughts, and actions toward others. Can I admit that I don't always know myself? I can confuse who I think I ought to be with who I am.

But, Lord, You know me better than I do. Please reveal to me the ways that are authentic for me. Lead me toward Your truths so I can rest in them and use them as my foundation.

Right Intentions

Rather, as servants of God we commend ourselves in every way: in great endurance; in troubles, hardships and distresses; in beatings, imprisonments and riots; in hard work, sleepless nights and hunger; in purity, understanding, patience and kindness; in the Holy Spirit and in sincere love; in truthful speech and in the power of God.

2 CORINTHIANS 6:4-7

Protect my role as a believer, Lord. Guard my reputation and my actions. Give me a cautious spirit so that I wait before I speak out. Preserve my intentions so that they are pure and righteous. Direct me toward the ministry that suits my gifts so I serve You well with unfailing devotion.

I long to be sincere as I serve You and serve others in the power You give to me.

May I Be Faithful

Now it is required that those who have been given a trust must prove faithful. I care very little if I am judged by you or by any human court; indeed, I do not even judge myself. My conscience is clear, but that does not make me innocent.

1 CORINTHIANS 4:2-4

When today is over, I hope You will have found me to be a true servant, that my actions have been pleasing to You and worthwhile for Your children. I pray You will find my heart to be right and faithful in the work I have done. My day is an offering to You that cannot be repeated. Only today will I have this particular set of circumstances. What I do with these opportunities reflects my belief in You.

Lord, I hope to do and go beyond what is required of me. At the end of this day, I hope to be a blessing to You, my Creator.

Motivated by Love

And now, dear lady, I am not writing you a new command but one we have had from the beginning. I ask that we love one another. And this is love: that we walk in obedience to his commands. As you have heard from the beginning, his command is that you walk in love.

2 JOHN 5-6

From the beginning of the day until the passing of the night beneath the stars, I pray that I follow the command that is born of Your will—to love one another. Give me Your heart for others so that my thoughts turn to compassion and unity rather than judgment and separation.

I pray for this day and all those to come...each one an opportunity to show You to the world and to show You my faithfulness. It is out of gratitude that I step into my morning. It is with humility that I turn to You throughout the day. Lead me with love so that I may follow in the path of love forever.